The 21st century
MERCENARY
OPERATIONS MANUAL

Vol. I - Introduction & Training

To those who think,

to those who dare,

to those who do,

to those who succeed.

Success is nothing more than taking advantage of an opportunity

- unknown -

"You are not superman"

- Franklin J. Camper, at the first page of his
Mercenary Operations Manual, released in 1986 -

A quote by a true mercenary legend to consider, before you
pick up a gun and travel the world.
A legend of a time gone by, at least that is what a lot of
people think had to admit that many of his students have
been involved in small scale wars all over the world. Even if
Franks professional background was subject to various
discussions, the fact that many guys that attended his
"Mercenary School" often went into mercenary work
afterwards is a widely known fact.

But aren't the times of these mercenaries gone? The guys
posing in warzone-pictures in the old issues of magazines like
"Soldier of Fortune" and "Gung Ho". Often unshaved, the
bare chest covered by some chest rig and sunglasses and an
old rifle giving the hint of danger, adventure and fortune.
Weren't those guys finally eliminated by the rise of the
modern private armies, the PMCs?
Not at all!
Of course, the market seems dominated by the big players
with the official website, own legal and PR professionals and
so on. Yet, the "old-school" mercs never vanished, for they
have a market the big players can't serve. It's too unofficial
for a company to work at, the fear of being seen there too
big, the stakes too high for anyone with a name. Or, too small
and specific to have experts for. Yes, big PMCs are dominating
the private war market today, yet never made the classic
mercenary type obsolete. As we will see in VOL. II, they can
be more of an asset and a potential customer - if you wish so.

Just don't give up on your merc-dreams by the chatter of some people in the social media communities and websites of the www claiming our trade to be dead and gone.

But don't hope for too many friends out there anyways. You are on your own, Joe Merc! as another legend of the community, Paul Balor, called his readers in his mid-80s „Manual of the Mercenary Soldier". To honor this war machine and legend, we will stick to this from now on. You don't like that? I don't care.
Better get used to shit like that for "you need the sensitivity of a crocodile" in this way of life, to quote him once again.

A lot has happened since Frank, Paul and some others wrote their books while travelling the world and shooting people for pay. The mentioned Private Military Companies (PMCs) founded, professionalizing big parts of the market in a way that didn't exist in centuries since the medieval age. The internet including the darknet and social media changed our communications and the easy-west conflict broke down (or so it seemed) only to be followed by the „Global War on Terrorism" since 2001.
But, looking more deeply, not that much changed at all. Small scale wars and guerilla conflicts all over the world, with thousands of unofficial: private fighters, mercenaries, soldiers of fortune, volunteers and the like going on nonstop. A steadily growing market for military skills and training even in the „developed" first world that ranges from military combatives training for street defense over combat survival training for preppers up to military sniper / designated defensive marksman and close quarter battle and room clearing training in privately owned sniper ranges and kill-houses for both fun and preparation, be it a home invasion or

„the end of the world as we know it".
Also, a growing demand in realism made movie and video game makers hire „military consultants", starting with some mustached merc calling himself *John Mullins* helping to develop the PC game „Soldier of Fortune" in the late 90s up to that former Navy Seal guy training Keanu Reeves for a fucking huge amount of time, bullets and money to become a „John Wick" even those of us in the trade admire for the skill shown on screen.
So, after all it seems that if you want to risk your life by pursuing an adventurous career as a gun for hire, there is work for you. More than enough!
But there is also the risk to get ripped-of, crippled, traumatized or, less fatal, financially ruined. And honestly, no person, course or book can eliminate those risks.

Yet, this book is intended to open your eyes to the pros and cons of the merc trade in today's world, opportunities, dangers and some solid, first-hand experience.

There is NO rational, logical reason why a citizen of a wealthy, prosper country would even think about living a mercs life – so I won't try to convince why you to do something like that and sacrifice a security and standard of living that never before existed in the world and that a lot of people dream about. Or risk your life for lousy food, restless nights, giant insects, sunburns and the chance of severe diarrhea or some bullet or IED causing even more discomfort.

It's a funny fact that exactly the same shit that makes people give up their lives and makes them become refugees begging and risking all they have for shelter in some better place often makes a few of us FROM that very "better place" leave it all behind and engage in the very war the others fled from.

Are we perverts, unthankful for our luck to be born in peace and wealth? Or are those others cowards, running instead of taking a stand for their home?

I don't know. And don't care.

Everybody is different. We differ in taste of music, movies, food, sex, and so much more. We also differ in acceptance of, and quest for danger, usually seen more by style of driving and hobbies. Some are drawn towards boxing, MMA, Bungee jumping and free climbing, some to building their RC train in the basement or growing Bonsai. That seems to be perfectly normal to most – why judge our different likings when it comes to war, to conflict and to danger.

I assume that the fact of you reading this manual shows that either you are thinking about doing it, already doing so or are, in some other way, interested in people living like that. Why … answer that to yourself, your girl, your macho-beer-buddies or your shrink.

All I can tell you is that, in my humble opinion, it beats spending your life in a cubical or in another boring place, making Netflix and video games the only excitement you have and turning you into a fat, unmanly, bored and unsatisfied Walther Mitty, dreaming to at least once in his miserable life to feel strong and masculine by fighting something else than his high body fat percentage.

For a chosen some of us, it's better to add some life to the days than days to the live. I'm NOT saying risking your life and health is the only way to do so. Not at all, there are countless. If after this manual you decide becoming a merc is NOT your way, don't ever think for a second I would think less of you, or would anyone else in this business that has half a brain.

We are not all IT guys! Not all are artists, musicians, actors, writers, leaders or organizers, womanizers or even interested in those. If this manual, in the end, gave you a laugh or two and helped you to decide informed, you are lucky and have my respect, no matter the decision.

It's the guys that go into this work WITHOUT deciding first, that realize in the field, worst of all in battle "I'm wrong here" that put all others in danger and are a pain in our asses.

So are the wanna-bees that claim they "would be THE #1 if not for" or even "did this, and then, and that…" in some forum or even out here in real life. So once more, don't feel bad when this trade, in the end, turns out to be not yours and you better go somewhere else to "fill your days with life!"

But I can almost see you thinking "NO! I'm just right here!" That's fine, we need more people in this trade, for there is work to be done – meaning there are wars to win, or at least to take part in.

But once more for the protocol:

All in information in this book is meant for informational purposes and without guarantees.

Any other use is NOT INTENDED and YOUR DECISION AND RISK ONLY! Also, laws are changing all the time and may change dramatically one minute after this is released. So, check with an attorney before you take any action that might be questionable. Same accounts for a visit to your MD before doing anything that may increase your heartrate and so on.

So: keep your head down and good luck, Joe Merc. There will be many times you're gonna need it!

Chris Ronson

INTRODUCTION

For those interested in the business of being a gun for hire, the average merc job seems only a little harder to find than a needle in a haystack, only difference being: the needle isn't necessary there at all.
In the social media and its forefathers, the forums, the answer to the question „How do I become a Merc?", formulated often full of hope and excitement, is usually: „Piss of noob! First, we are not Mercenaries but Private Security Contractors. Mercs don't exist anymore! Second of all, you need to have a high-end military background, combat arms or special forces, plus a XYZ citizenship, a valid fuckaduck123 security clearance etc. to even be CONCIDERED in the hiring process of those companies! So don't bother us with your shit, join the army or stick to „Battlefield", idiot!"

Other candidates interested in becoming a real soldier of fortune are scammed by „academies" and courses promising high paid armed overseas work for anybody doing this or that course – and paying it up front, please! And often, there is „only one more thing to be paid before that contract finally starts and the big bucks start coming in. Please transfer quickly…"
Only people here making money by their military and combat skills are usually the guys running the courses.

And all too often, individual believe the words written by some unknown guy, gal or whatever else people today identify as into the www, or get ripped off by a would-be merc-maker and leave disappointed, not knowing that there are hundreds of people, with and without a PMC contract or a shiny Delta Force background, making a living as a gun for hire, at home as well as abroad. Some are heavily paid – some are not, or at least not by the people they lend their arms and knowledge to. More on that in issue #2.

But if you are not one of the „lucky ones" chosen by a PMC but still lured by the thought to become a real mercenary, a gun for hire like those great guys in „the Expendables", minus the BS of course, be assured – it IS possible.
Not easy, or pleasant, or safe – but if it was, you wouldn't be interested, right?

So, Joe Merc, let me take you on the road to living a mercs life. A life on the edge, made of guns, tactical vests and sunglasses, money, bullets, heat, hunger and sometimes unreal craziness. And definitely one of the most exciting things to do in your few years on this planet.

Are you ready? Let's go!

A BRIEF HISTORY OF THE TRADE

To be prepared for the challenges and surprises in this line of work, a look into our past is a lot more valuable than one may think.

As long as humans existed, there has been war. Look anywhere in any time period and you will find people fighting each other over land, money, religion or whatever else reason they found. So, in my opinion it's only fair to say that war is as much part of being human as eating, drinking or having sex.

Also, you will see that in all times people paid others to fulfill any of those basic needs – war included. Whenever people lacked manpower, skill or just plain balls to go to war defending themselves or conquering more riches, they tended to find someone do it for them or at least support them in some way, in exchange for something these people wanted. So, it seems that our trade fills a basic human need.

Over the centuries, the details ranged from whole armies of ill-trained and ill-equipped masses of mercenaries meant to be spent on the battlefield, hired by kings with enough coin over specialists like the "Doppelsoeldner" in medieval Europe to sole individuals traveling the worlds wars for adventure, money and fame.
Let's have a closer look at the "Doppelsoeldner" (German for "double-mercenary"). They were paid double the amount others got, for their "Masters certification of the two-handed sword" a letter issued to them to prove their skill in using the huge, two-handed swords – also meaning they would be placed in the front rows of the battle formations.

Why is this of interest for you, even though you'll probably never touch any sword in your career? Because it shows a rule that is valid today as much as back in the days of swords and longbows:

Skills, especially those only a few have, ideally with prove in form of a certification, in combination with the will to take higher risks results in higher payment.

Well, don't rush out of the door in search of a teacher for the two-handed-sword now - demand isn't really big today. But keep the rule in mind!

Fast forward, some powerful people decided that honor and duty should replace financial payment in an army and this became the "new normal", ending up in two world wars that were fought almost without any hired guns. The "flying tigers" were the most prominent little exception.

After the second world war was over, the world changed again and with the "cold war" everything went back to small scale conflicts, irregular armies, militias – and Mercenaries. Africa and South America were real merc hotspots from the late 50's 'till the early 90's.

After 2001, the PMCs began to take over the market and what once was a shady, shadowy business became once more an official one.

Just like always, the world turned on. Wars ended only to give birth to new insurgencies. Al Qaida was relentlessly fought for years, swallowing countless dollars and lives – only to have the IS (or ISIS, or ISIL) rise as an even more powerful end terrifying terrorist organization. Also, Russia took the Krim and thereby started another small-scale war, this time in the Ukraine. So, you may see that things change, but war doesn't so much. And as long as there is war, there are opportunities to work there.

Terms and definitions — what exactly is a Mercenary?

Pinning down an exact definition for anything in this world is work that millions of scientists do when publishing, requiring to define any term that may be interpreted differently by different people for the work they publish.

Knowing this as well as the fact that war tends to have a „fog of war" with it and especially those that are not part of any regular outfit have an additional urge to not stand in the spotlights of the world's attention, while also tending to show a certain dishonesty regarding their reasons to take part in the hostilities makes a clear distinction and definitions extremely hard. Now add the fact that, thanks to Hollywood, comic books and Video Games, Mercenary is almost either an insult and often felt to be closer to „criminal" or „arms smuggler" or otherwise to "invincible super warrior" than „soldier" you will have a hard time finding somebody openly calling himself a mercenary. Same is true for Soldier of Fortune which is often used synonymous with „cheap adventurer " or associated with the video game series (that was in cooperation with the magazine by the way).

So? What exactly is a mercenary and what's the difference to a Soldier of Fortune, a Volunteer in a foreign army, a military advisor, international security consultant, a freelance tactical instructor that is teaching warfare-related topics for money or a Private Military Contractor. The last one is he only one that can be defined quite easily: A Private Military Contractor is a person owning a business of some kind allowing him to issue bills to a larger company he works for as a freelancer in

a war- or crisis zone, usually in an armed protective position or as an instructor. This concept allows the big company to bypass issues like social insurance and all the other stuff that would make it unpleasant to impossible to send an employee to a warzone, especially when issuing him or her a ballistic vest, a chest rig, an assault rifle and task that employee with a high-risk perimeter protection mission for up to 20 hours a day.
Yet, its way harder to distinguish the other descriptions of people taking part in war without being send there by their country or a official corporate contract.

To be honest, it's not harder – it's simply not possible. The terms are not universally defined. Example: a lot of left-wingers consider all of the western troops today „mercenaries ", because the western states pay their soldiers. Usually this is meant to intend the majority of those soldiers is in the forces for the sake of money, not idealism, the wish to protect the country etc.

And since, when it comes to war, killing and the like, people tend to be dishonest, especially regarding their motives, there isn't a 100% proof that this assumption is wrong.

Another definition of a mercenary is tried in a „Protocol Additional to the Geneva Conventions of 12 August 1949, and relating to the Protection of Victims of International Armed Conflicts (Protocol I), 8 June 1977":

Mercenaries

Article 47 - Mercenaries

1. A mercenary shall not have the right to be a combatant or a
prisoner of war.
2. A mercenary is any person who:
(a) is specially recruited locally or abroad in order to fight in
an armed conflict;

(b) does, in fact, take a direct part in the hostilities;

(c) is motivated to take part in the hostilities essentially by
the desire for private gain and, in fact, is promised, by or on
behalf of a Party to the conflict, material compensation
substantially in excess of that promised or paid to combatants
of similar ranks and functions in the armed forces of that
Party;

(d) is neither a national of a Party to the conflict nor a
resident of territory controlled by a Party to the conflict;

(e) is not a member of the armed forces of a Party to the
conflict; and

(f) has not been sent by a State which is not a Party to the
conflict on official duty as a member of its armed forces."

Being in this trade for some years, I have not met many guys that match that description. Point (b) for example excludes any PMC, because even the most seriously armed protective team will not „take a direct part in the hostilities" in common understanding. (That's by the way the main argument of our "official" freddies in the PMC business why they aren't mercs. They will fight being called mercenaries to their last breaths. At least against outsiders.)
As won't any foreign experts on weapons, tactics etc. So a bunch of former special forces soldiers could train the newly founded elite unit of some warlords army in everything from room clearing to demolitions and assassinations, run around armed all the time themselves, change the wars outcome by setting up that unit, therefore get paid a fucking ton of blood diamonds and still not be considered mercenaries. Makes sense, doesn't it?

So, let's consider this definition useless, shall we. Lacking a final answer that, as far as I'm concerned, only the god of war himself may have, let's keep it easy for this book:

Ignoring the quite easily defined PMC, let's just say a Merc, a SoF, the volunteer and all the others mentioned basically do the same thing: they take part in a war they are not sent to by their government. They fulfill tasks associated with military and warfare, from scouting and fighting to training, maintenance, consulting in matters related to warfare and the like.

For distinction, we will look at the motive and use the fictional „Tom", who left the safety of his job in a fast food restaurant to join a militia in some shithole and fights alongside them against some other militia.

If Tom was merely doing this for profits sake, either directly by getting paid in Dollars, Bitcoin or something else by the militia, or in less direct ways we will consider him a Merc.

If he basically is after the adventure of finally doing something „cool" in his life, his motivation is adventure. So, paid or not, he could be called a Soldier of Fortune.

If he joins because of his strong personal believes in the cause of the outfit he joins, we will call him a volunteer.

So, let's make it easy: Inside our circles, you can think of yourself and the rest of us as whatever you think. To me, anyone crazy enough to go out and put a price tag on his warfare-related skills, knowledge and experience is a mercenary. Outside of our little „family" we will ALWAYS stick to terms like „volunteer", „humanitarian aid worker", „consultant" and the like. So, your bank needs a reason to give you an account in foreign currency, airport officials ask for your reason of visiting or something like that - NEVER refer to yourself as a mercenary or Soldier of Fortune. As great Paul Balor once wrote „The Merc tag is a rea putdown in respectable circles – including the once who employ them. "

The Mercenary solution — now and back then

Mercenaries exist for millenniums now, making a lot of people considering us the second-oldest profession.

And that's right! Standing armies, formed of enlisted men (more or less) forced to fight and die for god and country were relatively rare if you look into our world's history a little more than in our previous chapter. What I suggest you to do! Believe me or not, those that survive in the mercenary world are usually a highly literate crew. Being dumb, uninformed or ignorant, without some NCO or Officer doing the thinking and planning for you, gets you killed quickly. At least, no government will have to release a press statement for your life's end somewhere.

So, why were mercs always there, you may ask? Simply because they were, and are, *desperately needed.*

Your private outfit, militia or other group requires military-kind knowledge and training?
Hire a merc!
A government can't do something with regular troops including their „black-ops" guys for political reasons or pure cowardness?
Hire a Merc!

A government unit is too restricted regarding its options in training and the knowledge is outdated? Fresh input is needed from a place called the free market, where innovation is key to success and professionals of all kind offer virtually

anything you may need?
Hire a merc!

A small or mid-sized company wants to do business in some shithole but can't afford those twelve high-end former SEAL operators the huge PMC offers as a minimum package?
Hire a merc!

A small outfit, rebel group, volunteer battalion or whatever in some shitty, pointless war somewhere is low on fighters, support people, subject-matter-experts, guns, supplies, knowledge … everything except for a cause worth to die for?
… well, you start to get it, Joe Merc, don't ya?

So, you see that there is plenty of work for you in the mercenary field, even without being a former whatsoever operator in Uncle Sam's or someone elses army. Even though it doesn't hurt to be.

But even i fit seems unlikely, believe me if I tell you that there were and are great Mercs out there, shooting and looting, that never served one day in an regular army.
Of course, service in a regular military offers a lot of benefits for starting a mercenary career: Knowledge of weapons and firing techniques, basic hygiene and survival, physical fitness and warfare itself. Also you are usually much more accepted when you've already got „some notches on your handle".

But as I said – it's not imperative. Also, it has some downsides, like being used to having almost everything sorted out for you. Paperwork, travel arrangements, places to sleep and eat, medical care... all a soldier has to do is whatever is ordered.

Let's ignore all the myths, the danger, glamour and so forth and just se FACTS:

A mercs work is a service, bought by a customer. So, military background or not, the mercenary needs to have SOMETHING TO OFFER THE EMPLOYER NEEDS!
That may be basic infantry skills, knowledge of supply chain management, some high-end cyber-warfare software, UAV handling, proficiency in a specific skill like room clearing, counter custody, interrogation, K9 aka Dog handling and training, knowledge of open-sea pirate attacks and how to prevent them, close protection, area and language knowledge, intelligence gathering, ... or just to be another dumbass holding a rifle in the next assault.

In a lot of cases non-military guys offer highly specialized knowledge, making them required by customers up to governmental outfits all over the world. Want an example?

Scott Bab adapted traditional Pilipino knife fighting based on large blades and machetes (Kali & Escrima) to smaller, modern blades, common in an urban environment while also including data from extensive research on knife attacks and - fights in modern day urban environments. Scott is a devoted martial artist with no noticeable background like being some former SWAT officer, CIA operative or shit.

Yet, his skills and the product based on them called „Libre" quickly got the attention of some specialized Mexican governmental outfits taking part in the grueling and merciless „war on drugs" that gets a lot more people killed than the rest of the world notices . They got the training and even reported back to Scott what „had worked" good, resulting in a dead or disabled cartel members – also allowing Scott to improve his product and service and also advertise with real-world tested knife combat. Highly valuable in a more and more pussyfied martial arts world with dojo ballerinas and overweight „masters" with zero experience in real violence everywhere.

So, can we consider Scott a merc?

Well: did he make money selling military / combat related skill to a foreign patron in need, without being motivated only by that patrons' cause?
So yes, even without shooting somebody Scott became a mercenary by selling skills in killing by knife to para-military units and, later, civilians alike. Libre will be subject later in this book again, but its already highly recommended to be checked out by anybody willing or merely interested in becoming a gun-for-hire. Like great Paul Balor once wrote: „In our environment, our violent lands, skill with a blade will win you acceptance you'd never get if you came in, say, as the world's foremost expert on submarine guidance systems." (Balor, P. - Manual of the Mercenary Soldier, P. 109)

Another prime example are paramedics providing extensive trauma first-aid training to foreign warriors in need of it. Guys that often start on a point where putting a band aid on somebody in need of it seems like rocket science. Making these guys handy with tourniquets, Israeli bandages, combat gauze and the like provides lots of them a good living, travelling the worlds warzones, assisting foreign forces and getting paid good money to do so.

So, Joe Merc, the market IS there – as long as you have something to offer to it, you're up for employment once you learn where to look and where not to.
If you don't have specific skills like a great knife fighting system, tactical medicine, close protection, logistics or the like – don't worry! We'll get you into some foreign war, too. You're just not going to start that nice, glamourous and well-paid a specialist can. Until, later, you become one.

But even if you already have a skill in demand out there, don't rush to the airport yet. Make sure that you live to spend it, as Frank Camper put it. Even if your job is „only" some sort of consulting, training or stuff like that – you NEED to be a warrior to make a living working in warzones. This is essential to both your overall acceptance and mere survival. Don't think for one second you'll be safe over there, wherever „there" is. Even if you decide to serve customers in peaceful countries with war-relevant training and knowledge: without the „edge" of a trained warrior capable to kill and survive, you're going to be considered a scammer, wannabe or the like soon. The modern world is awash with theorist! Even if killing people is not the primary service you're paid for – make sure you can do it anyway. A need will arise sooner or later if you live this way. That's for sure.

MORALS OF A HIRED GUN

This may be a shock, but contrary to public belief you're not free from any morals, laws and rules.

The reasons for this are several: first, your customer hires YOU as well as your skills and knowledge. If you have a reputation for being unprofessional, unstable, constantly drunk or high, criminal, violent towards allies or simply an annoying piece of shit you better have unique skill to offer. It's a small path you are walking too much of morals and concerns about laws and you are worthless too. Its literally a very grey zone we work in most of the time. As a simple example: crossing a border illegally may be needed at some point. A lot of warzones are officially restricted areas and won't let tourists in.

If you feel like breaking the law by illegally crossing the border is a no-go for you, think again about your motivation for this line of work.

If you, on the other hand, feel like using that skill to get some kilos of heroine in or out with you, you might be better of in another line of work again.
Killing is usually necessary at some point in this job and enjoying the thrill of a fight is okay. Some do, some don't. But enjoying killing so much that you start slaughtering innocents isn't. I hope that's not unexpected for you!
To give you another example: I once worked with a unit supposed for rapid deployment by helicopter. They were top fit, tough as nails types that spent most of the time waiting for the "go" in the weight room. Also, it was a known secret

that steroids, boosters containing amphetamines and the like were normal within the team. The competition who benched the most, ran the mile fastest and had the biggest arm was ever-present. But they got the job done, were world-class athletes and highly professional. Nobody cared until one day they got themselves some new booster from a local store (mistake) and tried it while waiting for a possible "go" to come (big mistake). The shit they took made them stop training after some minutes because the dosage resulted in severe cramps. They were literally unable to move. Now guess what... right! The command came that very moment and the mission had to be aborted because the team had consumed a questionable substance. The damage caused by this event lasted for years, resulting in a damaged reputation of the whole unit, investigations, punishment, increased controls and so on...

Hopefully, this will help you with your orientation in the future. As a mercenary, you are part gentleman adventurer and part savage. Keep the balance!

TOP 5 DON'Ts OF THE MODERN MERCENARY
If you still feel insecure or like having to be some Ned
Flanders, don't worry. You're allowed and expected, within
the mentioned limits, to be pretty much of an outlaw in this
job!
Just to give some more details on what to avoid, here are the
top 5 things you should avoid at all costs, based on personal
experience as well as research. Stay away from those and you
will find employment a lot easier - and enjoy showering
without being gang-raped in the future!

#5 smuggle, sell or consume illegal goods of any kind.

*#4 work for organizations considered illegal by UN, NATO,
EU or other big organizations. Especially terrorist groups and
drug cartels.*

*#3 Taking any work against your own government - or any
internationally accepted one.*

*#2 Attacking teammates, allies, or civilians in any way. This
includes bar brawling, except for unavoidable self-defense
when attacked!*

*#1 betraying, double-crossing or just bad-mouthing your
employer in any way. This also includes the time after the
contract!*

Regarding #4: keep in mind that "brave freedom fighters" can
become terrorists quickly sometimes. Research the US
support on the Taliban in the 80s for example and you'll see
that Uncle Sam sponsored a lot of the ordnance they got shot
with in the war that started in 2001. This means that you

should keep an eye on this sort of information if you work with any sort of "freedom fighters" - and make sure to leave if the need arises.

MERCENARY SKILLS

To survive in a warzone, keep all your limbs and mental health (relatively) existing and working and also make money doing so, requires a truckload of skills. Some obvious, some not so much. But all acquirable in a relatively short amount of time, given the will to suffer, sweat, read, listen, research, bleed and develop beyond expectations and even believes to become, literally, a war machine.

Given the fact you're still reading this book, I assume that the necessary will IS there. So, let me show you where to test if your desire to live your life as a soldier of fortune, a hired gun travelling a world full of money and guns, of women and danger, is strong enough.

Obviously a hired soldier will need skills commonly associated with a soldier in general: fitness, shooting, combatives, fieldcraft & survival etc.
One of the nasty little secrets of this trade is that a lot of guys, especially those with a background in the regular military, consider this enough. It isn't! At least if you want to maximize your chances of survival as well as your chances to become an asset to customers. The key is to add „softer" skills to your toolbox, skills that are usually associated more with intelligence personal than soldiers. Yet, you are not a soldier. As a freelancer, you will be moving and sometimes working in a more civilian environment. Often you will live closely to locals and other foreigners that fight for the side you work for. Language skills, blending into a scene, as well as some diplomacy, manipulations and maybe even the good stuff like interrogation and lockpicking may prove to be of great value

when working without a big department and several agencies
in the background.

BUT: always keep in mind that, in our tense times, you'll look
like a terrorist to a lot of people with the skills and knowledge
you will try to get. I know, that's unfair, so feel hugged.

And it's true that there are many skills similar. Same accounts
for governmental "black-ops" guys, but those are trusted
more because they are on an agencies pay list and usually
swore an oath to their country.
If you check closely, you'll see that for example, the 9/11
terrorists did a lot of trainings similar to those you'll be
advised to take. Also any terror-camp trainee will have
fitness, hand-to-hand combat, shooting, tactics and the like.
To some degree at least, believe me that the average terrorist
is hardly high-skilled. Most of the training given to these
fuckers in addition to indoctrination is meant to create
confidence rather than real skill. And if you consider their job
usually includes dying by either blowing themselves up or
fighting 'till death, you may guess why.
How likely you are to be suspected as a terrorist depends on
your looks a lot: nope, I'm not a racist, but many people are
to some degree. So, if you have brown eyes, dark hair and
maybe even a beard, you are much more likely to be
considered a potential thread to freedom than the average
Caucasian. But don't feel to safe as one of the latter: with a
rise in right-winged terrorism (like Utoya and Christchurch) a
white male too interested in the wrong stuff may result in
very interested officials as well. Remember the pages about
morals?
Once you've been suspect to allegations like that, consider

this job a LOT harder. From finding work (meaning someone willing to risk working with a terror suspect) to international travel and even financial transactions – you'll soon discover the power of our governments in the global war on terror. What can you do to prevent this?

OPSEC

If you have no military background, you most likely never heard the term OPSEC. Well, now you did and its much more than a term: its your new lifestyle from this very day until you die!

Being an acronym for "Operational SECurity" the application of this principle is universal. Keeping your mouth shut towards outsiders is one major part of it.

So, no matter how excited you are about your choice of becoming a gun for hire, or your first combat shooting course or whatever, don't run around and tell it to everybody else. This includes your current job, friends and sports club as well as the www and social media.

Always keep in mind that mercenaries to most people belong into the same realm as hitmen, terrorists and the like. Imagine this for a minute: after three months of CrossFit and boxing (more on this later) you start to get more and more attention in your office: you visibly lost about 10 kg of fat while some muscles appeared. Also, your body posture became taller and a lot more confident. That's a lot of change and people usually are afraid of change. If you now start telling everyone about that "great combat shooting course you went to" and that "awesome knife combat training with that former SWAT guy..." you're likely to have them talk about you A LOT more. And not necessarily only the "he's so cool" talk. One of your colleagues, say Mr. Adam Sheeple, may find your changes and your interest in weapons and martial subjects so disturbing that he feels like reporting it to someone he knows... and suddenly you have an early visit from local police.

Same accounts for your online activities. The "shemag-and-AK" pic may be enough to get you a visit and an investigation.

Remember, all the school and office shootings as well as the global terrorism, combined with the medial impact of those, got people VERY touchy in things like that.

Always consider what you may look like to others and adapt accordingly. You won't be able to hide your increase in fitness, but the answer "I saw that movie about the diseases associated with overweight" or "I felt a strong need to become stronger, healthier and more confident" won't cause anyone to worry about you planning to shoot up your co-workers someday.

When it comes to more specific training like PMC or CP courses, combat first aid and the like, the I-love-fitness-now stuff won't work. But even here you are advised to be careful regarding your intentions. Self defense taken seriously because of the recent increases in crime in your neighborhood, just wanting to live out your Jason Bourne fantasies before its too late, an interest in changing the job and getting into close protection work... all this is okay.
"I plan to become a mercenary" will be problematic even with a lot of guys from our business.

Another thing: always assume especially your online activities being watched, at least to a certain degree. No agency has the manpower to manually scan all the data that we produce online, but several programs (we'll simplify here a lot!) of several services check for specific things.

Yes, you probably bought this book on Amazon. I'm pretty sure of that because it's released there. Don't worry, people buy a lot of shit there.

But buying too many books, videos and other stuff there that is related to urban warfare and explosives may result in somebody starting to have a closer look at you. Same accounts for downloading old books about building explosives, guerrilla warfare and the like. Doing this on a smartphone or laptop registered to your name and from your home wifi may not be the brightest of ideas...

Summary: learn to keep your mouth shut and your business to yourself. Think in advance of a believable reason for your interests and activities and consider that the person you speak to may be very afraid of domestic terrorism, lone-wolf active shooters and the like. And also has friends in several agencies, interested in preventing the next Christchurch. That means, you prevent too: prevent being suspicious as much as you can. Any investigation focusing on you regarding serious crime, terrorism or psychological problems can cause you a lot of trouble later!

Physical Fitness

Surprise, surprise Joe! There is a reason all those great people making a living fighting others are in peak shape, no matter if they are soldiers, police S.W.A.T. officers, close protection operators or even professional full-contact martial artists. War and fighting are PHYSICAL, meaning that fitness is imperative for survival.

Assuming you're without any military or other relevant background: don't believe that a single-digit bodyfat percentage or those nice-looking veins on the biceps peak are required – or sufficient. They are definitely nice, yet not a must, and so are gyms in general.
Sprinting from cover to cover under fire, being clinched with somebody you want to kill and who wants to do pretty much the same to you, carrying ammo or another fighter, ... this is a fitness not acquired ideally by following some routine from the latest issue of „Muscle & Fitness" in your local gym or signing up in some „30 day abs for office workers" class next door.

Functional training is perfect for your needs, CrossFit being the most well-known, yet by far not the only, example of it. But if you can handle the sometimes cult-like feeling about their "boxes" and the people inside (that tend to appear a little bit like Scientologists on roid-injections) you have found a perfect place to get the kind of fitness you need.

Sprints, Burpees, Jumps, flipping tires or hitting them with a sledge hammer and other high-impact anaerobic fun (meaning your body produces energy anaerobically = without oxygen... means you wanting to puke and collapse, if you're not used to that. It's the nasty big brother of aerobics, like jogging, walking or the like) alternating with heavy compound lifts, addressing literally all muscles in your body and make them work together (instead of isolating them like in bodybuilding), medium and long distance cardio like running, biking, rowing and a shitload of other challenges like pushups, squats, situps, pullups, skipping rope, climbing ropes and so on.

That disgrace you call a body will quickly transform in a way healthier and combat-ready physique. Also, those full-time killers you will meet in a warzone will likely be way less motivated to enjoy your lovely, chubby man-boobs instead of your service if you appear fit and confident to take care of any shit that may come.

(If you happen to be a woman, the same applies of course. War knows NO gender. Yet, be prepared to be molested a lot more even when in top shape.)

Combat Strength Training, founded by a former Delta guy called Pat McNamarra is also a great source to check out. If you don't happen to live in the US or feel interested enough to book a flight to pay his live courses a visit, you can buy the program online.

Its designed from the very ground up as a fitness concept for warriors, developed and sold by a very experienced one – 22 years in special ops gotta mean something.

Funnily, the origins of the program root back to the fitness concept developed for the legendary „Delta Force" - by a civilian! He was hired to adapt the unit's fitness training to their mission's needs, and he wasn't even a SpecOps guy or something himself – no, DELTA hired an American Football coach. Well, sprinting in full kit while also being able to deliver for a longer period of time while also being tangled up with other guys full-force... they had a reason to estimate that guy the right advisor in matters of job-oriented fitness. Even though that coach was a true patriot and thereby refused to get paid, the story itself (told by Pat in his online course), is another example of a civilian getting hired to provide specialized service to a war-involved customer in need of his special knowledge or abilities.

Also, there are dozens of books out there by guys like Stew Smith (former Navy-SEAL) or Mark Lauren as well as stuff issued by units themselves, aimed to help the much-needed young human-capital for the next wars.

So, once you've done your research start by having a honest look at your current level of fitness and knowledge on how to perform the exercises required in an effective and safe way. Remember, doing fast and wrong pushups ,till you jam a shoulder or fumbling around with a heavy kettlebell until it falls and shatters your foot won't get you closer to a third world warzone. Instead, it may end what might have been a profitable and exiting career as a mercenary.
So: seek training by somebody qualified. Yes, that's usually NOT for free. Swallow it, buttercup. Being cheap on this end will leave you battered, broken and in a worse physical condition than you started with.

At least some staff guy at your local Golds Gym or whatever should explain you the basics like joint extension, breathing, avoiding injured necks, torn chest muscles and the like best you can.

Even better, he may work out a plan for your goals with you. Remember: better don't tell him you want to become a mercenary. Stick with being interested in joining the army, firefighters or just being more prepared and capable in an emergency. Functional Training became quite a craze since Y2K and chances are good that even in that gym around your corner, you'll have access to tools and knowledge in reality-oriented fitness.

Another option is to seek personal training by some guy skilled in topics like fitness and nutrition and maybe even military training. You may be lucky and already know that kind of guy or find him on craigslist, ebay or something like that. Just know that there are also a lot of wannabees and fraud artists out there, so that's not the ideal way.

Finally, you may invest time and money to become an expert yourself by taking a course for fitness trainers. But be warned Joe, a lot of bad providers around here again, giving you little more than shit in exchange of that precious money of yours.

„Why can't you just tell me where to go, Chris?" I see that question on your face right now. Well, two reasons:
First of all, I don't know where the fuck you are - or when, given you may read this a hundred years from now. Paper tends to last. So even though I may appear as some messiah-like uber-human, I can't foresee the place and time of you reading this. So, any specific address would be pointless.
Even more important, I want you to survive pursuing a mercs way of life. Anything else would be bad for my sales - dead mercenaries don't tend to recommend this book to others interested. So, I need to equip you with the skills necessary to survive in a world of chaos, deception and lethal violence. Being able to do your own research is one of them, even if it's

less cool than assaulting a building or silently killing some armed and armored jerk with your knife.

Intelligence is crucial to success in war, and lacking a big, overpaid intelligence agency like any military has at hand, you better know how to get information yourself. And here, only some bucks depend on your intel-gathering skill – not human live. So, go ahead.
Check search engines on the www., look after reviews, scan ads in the newspapers, make contact in a supplement store or just ask the next fit looking lad you meet for a place and trainer to go. Just make sure he won't take your questions as hint of sexual interest – unless, of course, it is.

Long story short: get the fuck of your ass and start working until you have a warrior's body, capable of ruck marches, climbing, fighting, sprinting and anything else war may throw at you.

When are you ready? Well, almost every special forces unit has their fitness test published online, again enabling the next generation to prepare better. For you as a gun-for-hire in training, these will also be a nice checkup. Just use common sense when choosing a test to orient at:
Unless you plan to do merc-work as a specialist on scuba-diving instruction, helping the "Liberation Army of Assfuckistan" to get their own SEAL-Unit, chances are slim you need to be much of a swimmer. Being able to not drown when falling of a boat will do. So, when choosing the world-famous fitness test of the US Navy Seals BUD/S training for example (a great test), don't care to much on the swimming part. If you do the test in your local gym, just do some rowing

on the machine or simply something like 50 – 100 squats instead. Just make sure to tire your big muscles a bit like that swimming would (to a guy swimming at least three times per week for 26 weeks straight preparing for that test as suggested by the SEALs themselves). But, being a nice and humble person, I worked it out for you to just try:

Navy US Navy SEAL fitness test (Gym-trapped-Mercenary edition)

After a brief warmup (say: run or bike 5-10 minutes, moderate speed) start with the first event. Rest exactly two minutes (no second longer, you lazy jerk!) and start the next one. Transfer by walking to the next event, when needed, is done in the REST periods!

EVENT	MINIMUM	GOOD
2 miles row (machine)	15:00	12:00 or less
Pushups (max. in 120 sec.)	42	80 or more
Sit-ups (max. in 120 sec.)	50	80 or more
Pull-ups (hanging free)	6	10 or more
1,5 miles run (treadmill or street)	12:30	10:00 or less

Sure, a lot of soldiers from just anywhere don't come close to these standards and still fight in wars. Why do you have to be that over-the-top? Simple answer: you are not part of the flock of radio-controlled rifle-firers called „Soldiers" today. You need to be able to survive all by yourself should the need arise – mediocrity won't be enough for the life you're after! If you want to just „do ok ", stay home in that cubical office.

MERCENARY COMBATIVES

A lot we said about fitness also can be applied when it comes to combatives, hand-to-hand fighting in life-and-death situations! And again, YES, you need that skill, even if acquiring it is likely to hurt your body and ego. A lot. Often.

„But I'm going to be a merc, Chris! Most likely gonna have a gun to shoot the bad guys. Why bother with some odd pyjama wrestling or shit?"

Well, Joe, first of all getting experience in H2H combat is going to improve your mindset. You're going to become a lot more confident and tough with some experience in fighting up, close and personal. Also, your anaerobic energy system (details in the previous chapter) will be tested.
Third of all, any weapon may fail, be empty or just not be there when the enemy is. Remember, your means of transport in and out of the place you're working are most likely to be civilian. As will be those precious rest and recovery times in Thailand or somewhere else. And both Bangkok and that economy-class seat in the Boing 747 are just not a good place to have any firepower with you, especially if a longer visit to a high-security prison is not on your holidays-to-do list.

Also, sometimes even on the job you won't get a weapon – but be sure you will have people disliking your presence and being overt about that.

So, Joe, no way around doing what any special forces soldier is doing, too: get some ass-kicking skills.

Starting with a can of something to drink and documentaries like „Human Weapon" or „Fight Quest" on Systems like Krav

Maga (H2H system of the Israeli military) or MCMAP (currently the H2H training of the famous US Marine Core) may be a good point to start, giving you an idea what to expect.

Striking and kicking, breakfalls and rolls, blocks, holds, throws, chokes as well as techniques to free from holds, techniques to disarm an attacker trying to kill you or threaten you with a knife, gun or stick (or, maybe, an a hatchet, axe, chain or the like) will be a part of a good training. As will be techniques to control a suspect in case a interrogation is necessary instead of a corpse, methods of using knifes, sticks and improvised weapons effectively yourself, silently taking out a guard with a knife or bare hands. The very best of those trainings will also teach you skills like verbally deescalating a conflict with one of your own guys, speaking a person to the ground when having a gun, teamwork with a partner or handcuffing and searching a person or even resist and counter attempts to control and arrest you. The latter may spare you some ripped-out fingernails, spikes driven into parts of you, being burned or having your head cut-off in front of a camera streaming the event live to make a statement and giving those at home that still know and care about you something to pay a shrink for.

Again, this market is full of wanna-bees, pussies claiming to be world-class-warriors, former special forces soldiers and some more. I admit, its hard to identify quality here when new to the material. Yet, there is a good point to start when you got literally no experience:
Boxing or Muay Thai (=striking) plus Judo or Brazilian Jiu Jitsu (=grappling)!
Yes, both are sports and NOT military or street oriented H2H fighting system. Yet, if you researched those military systems

as advised in the beginning oft he chapter, you may have noticed that almost every modern military combatives training is based on boxing strikes, kicks as also used in Muay Thai, Karate or Tae-kwon-do, and throws, chokes, holds and breakfalls from Judo and/or BJJ.

Those systems focus on REAL fights, even if they happen in a ring with a referee and rules, make them a great starting point. Training fights aka sparring is soon going to give you a feeling for what works and what it is like to fight somebody trying his or her best to defeat you. Making it a great tool for developing resistance to stress happening in a real fight. And yes, the first bullets coming your way, send by somebody you can't expect one bit of mercy from is stressful as fucking hell. Even if sparring is only, say, 10 % of that – better preparation than zero.

After something close to six months training your chosen striking and grappling style (at least twice a weak – each! Didn't think you're going to be taking names in split seconds, without a weapon, is a skill you can just acquire too easily, huh?) the chances of any would-be human-weapon, self-named expert and all the other human garbage filling the worlds martial arts schools and seminars to a huge degree is a lot less likely to be able to fool you. You will notice if that technique of grabbing the punching or stabbing arm is going to work because you received and delivered punches for real, intended to hit hard, with a real opponent doing the same.

At the same time, you learned basic skills also relevant in real-world combatives like non-telegraphic striking, choking someone unconscious or falling to the ground without breaking your bones.

So, while ideally continuing your striking and grappling, look for competent instructors in a more reality-oriented fighting style. Ideally, they will have a military or law enforcement background. Again, remember a lot only pretend to have, or they spent 12 years in the military, sitting in the back office and made coffee for the general. So, don't get fooled by somebody telling about all the bodies he stacked back then when he was a Marine – trust your own experience).

Krav Maga is still a very good choice if you happen to find courses with a good instructor. Sadly, those became rare diamonds since around 2012 when KM became an international business and everybody wanted a piece of that cake.

Check out Lior Offenbach and Itay Gil online to get another impression of how the good guys work – those that have „been there and done it" for real. Real KM, being used in Israel fighting terrorism daily, is a great choice and also you will have another advantage: developed in Slowakia in the 1930s and later developed further in the new-founded state of Israel, the system is based on strikes from boxing and falls, throws and holds from Judo while being simplified to be taught to soldiers with little time and prior skills to be applied in real life situations. So, your experiences from Boxing, Judo, Muay Thai etc. can be directly used within the system.

And, by the way, spare me that political bullshit about oppression of Palestinians or whatever.

That discussion is going on forever leading nowhere. If you have moral issues using a battle-tested concept or weapon because you don't agree with the political origin of it, better forget this whole Merc-thing and get back to pushing papers or something.

Combatives; as taught by Kelly McCann; and the Urban Combatives based on the teachings of Lee Morrisson are great sources to get some training at, too. And yes, you may now work those research skills of yours again.
[By now, you should feel at least not totally out of your comfort zone when working the www for information. Amongst spooks, spies and all those services that usually have a name made by three letters, this is called OSINT, meaning Open Source INTelligence. Believe me or not, even for those doing nothing but gathering information (say our beloved services like C-I-A), OSINT including the www, newspapers, TV etc. usually it's he most heavily used source, way more often than the cool stuff like double agents, high-resolution spy satellites and UAVs aka drones. Some day you will come across a real intelligence officer – this way of life is making that quite a safe bet. Assuming he is on friendly terms with you (or at least it seems like that) feel free to ask him about that. Maybe, he will answer. And maybe, that answer will even be the truth.]

Good training will include full-force-full-speed drills as well as techniques, as mentioned above, countering weapons, using them or just taking out an opponent even if he is totally high on drugs and no longer feeling any pain. Fighting several opponents will be trained, as well as attacking the targets most forbidden in any combat sport including the eyes, the throat, the balls, the knee joints or the back of the head with the body part causing the most damage while being least likely to be injured doing so: fingerstrikes to the eyes, hammerfists to the back of the head (likely to cause severe, lasting brain trauma) or a knife hand to the adams apple.

The "Face mash" is another great example of those simple-but-effective combatives:

Imagine standing in front of some really aggressive crackhead, hands up and palms facing him as you try to calm him down. As you realize the futility of your efforts, you burst off your rear foot towards him, your right hand formed like holding a big grapefruit. And that invisible grapefruit … you drive straight through his face!

Effects: your palm hits the nose, breaking it for good, and head with all your body movement behind it. The guys head gets hell of an impact, also likely to injure his neck. Your fingers are nicely spread, so one is likely to get into one eye. And best of all: you're not going to break your wrist or even get swollen knuckles.

While effective methods of combat-training are a requirement for this part of your training, always keep an eye for the other bad extreme: there are those instructors and students either so damaged by real-life experience or so driven by their egos that people taking the training are in danger to be seriously injured. Like in fitness, this is NOT acceptable! You're supposed to train to get ready for your career as a mercenary and improve your chances of survival – not to end it before it started by receiving serious brain damage or a stiff knee.

Sure, accidents can and eventually will happen when people start moving their bodies, no matter if its jogging, lifting weights, playing soccer or training to kill with nothing but their hands. Bur because of that very reason, the instructor should take every precaution possible to minimize the risk of injuries worse than a bleeding nose, bruises and a hurt ego. This includes protective equipment like protection glasses, groin protectors and so on as well as sorting out students that repeatedly hurt others or put them in danger by not obeying safety rules.

And don't believe for a second that bullshit some will tell you on how to „train as you fight" and how ist even harder in the military. Believe me, Joe Merc, that even the most tough units on this planet will make sure to minimize injuries in training best they can. In fact, the more „elite" the unit, the more so. Every single soldiers training in the military, especially in the special forces, cost a fucking lot of money and is meant to be used against the enemies of the state of that soldier – not to turn out having been in vain by crippling that guy for live and rendering him of no more use in war.

Regarding that „train as you fight" stuff: as long as you don't find a firing range that offers you a course firing real bullets on real humans that also have guns and shoot at you – your training will never be exactly like the fight. That's why its TRAINING after all!

That saying means to keep the goal (the real fight) in your focus in training and not get drawn away by irrelevant stuff like perfecting that isolated biceps-curl originating from bodybuilding and of little use anywhere except for the stage of a bodybuilding-show or maybe a beach with some hot girls or, another example, training the draw of your pistol from an IPSC sports holster instead from something you are way more likely going to carry some day in Shitholeistan while working.

Any training has to offer an experience as close to the real thing as possible, including exhaustion and pain, without putting the trainees in unnecessary danger doing so. Yapp, that IS a small edge to walk on – and that's why REALLY GOOD instructors are a rare and usually well-paid breed in

the world of warfare.
Remember that well, maybe you just got another possible option when selling yourself out there on the international market for mercenaries, soldiers of fortune, military consultants, PMCs, rouge as well as seemingly-rouge operators, international volunteers and all the other kids that play in the worlds less developed sandboxes.

Melee Weapons

The last chapters pointed out the difficulties of getting suitable fitness- and hand-to-hand-combat training in preparation to work as a hired gun.

Now, let me tell you that finding serious and useful training regarding knifes, batons and other melee weapons usually is even more challenging. Especially knife fighting is being considered an „evil" and almost „forbidden" subject, especially when the techniques and tactics included are effective, meaning methods to quickly kill an opponent or at least seriously injure him to stop him killing you.

That nasty reality, combined with the fact that the majority of knife wounds, even potentially lethal ones, tend to not be noticed by the person that gets hit boils down the options to combatively use a knife to a few especially brutal ones, including „shocking" the opponent by twisting the knife inside the wound after stabbing, attack the eyes and facial area or stab vulnerable parts of the body like neck or abdomen in a way best compared to a sewing machine, let alone stabbing someone's groin or anus. Not exactly the kind of stuff average joe wants to see or think about in his recreational time.

So, the least you should do to get some knowledge on using a knife in life and death combat is read the very short but extremely valuable „Put 'em down, take 'em out", written by Don P. who claims to have spent a long time in prison, gathering knife experience there – no way to confirm that, but his understanding of the subject made a lot of people consider him telling the truth. Including me.

If you want to get some hands-on training, look for courses in „Libre", mentioned earlier in this book.

„Piper" is another nice option, originating from South Africa and focusing on quick and deceptive movements with the knife, aiming to set up a quick and brutal killing strike. Or several.

Other than that, there isn't much internationally available knife training on the market.
The traditional arts usually take a long time to master and are often „softened" a little to attract more paying customers that want to do something cool as a hobby, not face the often disturbing reality of bladed combat.

When it comes to impact weapons like batons, the market looks a little better. Courses on the use of blunt weapons are offered mostly for security personnel, yet these are usually more reality oriented than traditional arts that waste your lifetime in endless drilling-loops when all you want is a basic knowledge on how to save your ass with an impact weapon.

If the concept taught is way more complicated or artistic that the following quote from „Put 'em down, take 'em out" on the use of blunt weapons, the system in question may be great for fitness, keeping a tradition alive or a spiritual development, but not to fight for your life in some dark ally in some even darker place on earth:

„Hit him in the head until he's dead!"

There may be additional stuff to non-lethal application, drawing, blocks and so on ... all fine. Once they start to play around and things get complicated and you find yourself fumbling like "where to put that now in step 6" you've definitely left the realm of reality-focused training.

FIREARMS TRAINING

No matter what kind of job or service you plan to offer to your employer – being handy with firearms and their use in combat is nonnegotiable for a mercenary. Be honest, guns are at least one reason you consider this career at all, don't you?

However, it's not enough to score maximum points with your favorite pistol or rifle static on a 25 yard bullseye target. Basic marksmanship is EXTREMELY important, yet it's only the mere foundation of your needs.
Knowing how to operate the most common guns in the third world, like the AK 47, the FN-FAL, the H&K G3 or the Dragunov SVD is important. So are skills like emergency and tactical reloads, fixing malfunctions in a way also working in the darkest of nights and after 36 hours with no sleep or food at all, drawing your pistol when the rifle has a jam including an understanding when and why this is used, shooting from cover, moving inside buildings, working with a partner and many more.

The market for training like this varies greatly from country to country, the USA, Israel, Poland, the Ukraine and South Africa having several schools that offer combat-relevant firearms training at acceptable prices. Some will also include so called force-on-force training, meaning the use of paint ammo against other people, giving you an even more detailed (and painful) impression of the differences between shooting some paper target and a moving, thinking and shooting human being.

So, start with some courses to cover basic pistol and rifle marksmanship, ideally with guns named above. Also, some training with common hunting rifles will make sense, because those are quite common in the warzones out there, too. And drop those cool aimpoints, EOtechs and all other stuff for now. It's time for iron sights, pal. Most of the aiming devices so beloved to the gun nuts in our home countries are worth more than an average wage for the guys in the lands that mercenary work will usually take you. So, don't expect to get some high-end scoped, shiny new weapon.

However, the biggest mistake is one a lot of people do – ranging from police guys, soldiers and competitive shooters up to all those wild cards out here. And that mistake is trying to run before being able to walk.

If you want to be really good (and reading this means you plan a career where your choice is to be good or dead) always hone the basics!
I know, training room-clearing with fog and strobes is cool. Yet, it all comes down to the fundamentals of sights, breathing, trigger control etc.

DRY TRAINING should be a constant in your life from this day, assuming you know what you do. If not, get of your ass and get real-life instruction!

If real guns are unavailable to you in your everyday life, don't worry! Good airsoft's are just as good as the real thing when it comes to honing the fundamentals in constant, thoughtful dry exercises.

After getting the fundamentals right, the options seem endless and to a certain point, it's up to you. A specific course for PMCs may be a wise investment for both skills and contacts. Good courses will cover stuff like team tactics, debussing from a vehicle, use of cover, shooting on the move and much more. You may also opt for DDM, designated defensive marksman, courses if working with a scope seems like a nice idea to you. CQC/CQB training, usually inside of a so-called „kill house" is also a great way to improve.

When it comes to heavier weapons like belt-fed machineguns, the options for training get very limited outside of the military and our planets lovely warzones.
Las Vegas and a few other places in the US and VERY few eastern European countries offer the experience to train with real machineguns or anything bigger. Also, the amount of ammunition needed and the small amount of competition in this field ensure prices stay high.
Good news is: this kind of course would make a nice bonus but isn't necessary. If you are handy with magazine-fed, semi-automatic rifles and pistols, maybe even shotguns and scoped rifles, you're good to go. Believe me that a lot of soldiers aren't trained in special weapons either. I met tons of guys from combat units all over the world that never even touched a rocket launcher and also had little experience in belt-fed toys. Of course, this differs widely from country to country. Yet, as a merc you will do fine to focus on the stuff recommended above, for it will be most available in the places we work. Also, you will likely get some "on the job" training sooner or later with the big guns.

One last word:
The basic training consisting of basic safety, sights, breathing, shot placement, fixing stoppages and so on should be done in a big and renown school (yapp, research goes again).
When the more „tacticool" courses come to play, know that a lot of schools also serve as recruitment centers for foreign

fighters. Also, the safety regulations may be ... different from what you consider normal. So better don't go there before you can handle yourself as well as your tools of trade. This fact also holds a potential way to get into the game, details on this including an example will follow in Vol. 2. Until then, get your ass in shape, so you will be interesting for these guys to hire – and good enough to survive and spend that first money earned as a merc.

Explosives

Life isn't fair, Joe Merc. That's for sure. I mention this fact to prepare you for a major disappointment: there is little chance to get serious training regarding explosives in civilian schools.

The topic is too "terroristic" for even the most liberal laws to allow. But I wouldn't dare to leave you with only this, don't worry. Just don't expect any secrets regarding civilian "how to build a charge and blow up a bridge" courses. This training exists in the militaries and terror camps of the world, the latter are hopefully not an option you consider. No, not even "just to learn this stuff and understand the enemy". You're going to be persona-non-grata in this business at best afterwards, a prisoner in a secret facility untouched by sunlight, attorneys or this "basic human rights" thing at worst.

The best start outside of MIL or LE will be some counter-IED training (IED = improvised explosive device) as many close protection and security schools offer. This is the easiest to find regarding all things BOOM. You'll get a good basic understanding of the topic here; typed of explosives, types of ignition, blast radius, shrapnel … even if you're not blowing anything up yourself.

The darker side of the internet offers thousands of manuals on how to build explosives of all kind. They range from books published in the 80s to stuff that was released by terrorist organizations themselves or authors claiming to be part of them. Besides the "terrorist" factor if you fail on OPSEC and get caught with any of that stuff, these sources also tend to be unreliable as hell. The described method of manufacturing an explosive may result in you blowing yourself up even when

you stick 100% to the recipe. So, read some of the material if
you want to, but don't take ANYTHING in there for real. Even
if you find matching methods in different sources – that may
prove it's a working way or that the authors copy from each
other.
Long story short: don't ever think of manufacturing ANFO or
any of that shit.

When it comes to hand grenades, things look better. The real
HE (high explosive) are of course unavailable to the public, yet
here we have a little trick: you can train the handling (basic
throw, throwing inside a room in a CQB situation and the like)
in many places using airsoft grenades. This also allows you to
not loose life, eyesight or limbs if you do any mistake. If you
are lucky enough to build a good relationship with a former or
active duty soldier trained in this stuff, you may learn all this
from him. If not, you're free to read the legally free-to-
download Field Manuals of the US Army for advice on
technique and handling and study the topic yourself.
Also, several CQB courses around the world use specific
fireworks to train throwing flashbangs. I recently did a course
in Poland where they had over-expensive but totally lovely
"Granat hukowo - błyskowy" firecrackers that also handled
like a real flashbang (ignited by ripping of a ring) and also
produced a bright flash. Well, having them thrown at you
every morning during your pre-breakfast run and obstacle
course was fun as well...

A last option may be some sort of civilian "fireworkers
licence" training. The legality of this kind of stuff varies
greatly and even with the license you probably won't be able
to stockpile C4 in your wardrobe legally. But the license and
the training to get it will give you in-deep knowledge on

explosives, ranging from the difference between burning and exploding to the pressure that different stuff creates, options of ignition and much more. But that's usually expensive, takes time and effort and may also make you subject to some security agencies attention and repeated checks. Which isn't really helpful in this job.

To summarize: basic counter-IED training is a MUST for our job - this shit is common in todays wars, in the hot zones as well as in our "peaceful" home countries. Handling grenades is also a good skill to have and not too hard to learn. All else is too dangerous to consider for now. Just like the machine guns and rocket launchers, you will find a lot more options once you're good enough to get into a conflict zone.

Awareness training

One of the most difficult to explain, yet lifesaving skills: Awareness, actively noticing your surroundings and scan for possible threats while at the same time does not wear yourself out unnecessary by paranoid behavior.

In the 1960s, a former US Marine and pioneer for modern combat shooting named Jeff Cooper developed a color code to make the abstract subject of awareness more tangible.

His COOPER COLOR CODE consists of four colors (sometimes in the police, there is „Black" as a #5. We will stick with the basic here.)

WHITE describes a status of NO ATENTION given to a person's surroundings at all. Correctly, the FBI also calls this the "victim state" because the majority of victims, crimes from theft and physical assault up to abduction, rape and murder, tend to state that the attacker „appeared out of nowhere" and that „everything happened so fast". This proves that the victim did not give its surroundings any attention for in most cases, the attackers didn't even hide. They just spotted an easy victim because of the lack of attention shown Don't be that victim, least of all in some 3rd world place where most people couldn't care less about you living or not

YELOW is the color for RELAXED ATTENTION. This is best explained with a usual, experienced person driving a car. With no signs of potential danger present, a driver usually will still look for something that may be of relevance – but without any tension or fear. To use this outside of the car and in a more violent context, replace road signs, trash on the street and places likely to have children run onto the street with people looking out of place, cover, escape routes and other things of relevance to your successful survival in an emergency. That's about it.

ORANGE means TENSE ATTENTION. If you spot a suspicious person (or more than one) heading your direction, you are moving towards a position where mines and boobytraps are likely to be set up, someone in the same room starts to look around nervously while reaching into his jacket... something indicating a potential threat means your status switches to orange. That's the moment to formulate a simple plan of action or even prepare for an encounter by hiddenly drawing your own weapon, moving to a better position etc. Also, you start to turn up your level of perception to the maximum

RED means that A THREAT IS PRESENT. Shooting, an explosion or „only "some drunk motherfucker trying to beat the shit out of you... RED means that you have to act. Hopefully you were able to spot the problem in advance and use the „orange "seconds to form a plan of action, ready your weapon or do something else to prepare instead of being totally surprised.

There are courses that add practical exercises to that concept and result in quick improvements of awareness and perception. Good close protection courses usually do, so do the better courses in realistic self-defense. If you have the option, take one.
One way or another: make being „yellow" a habit.

This sums up all skills needed to survive and work in the field, no matter if you're out on patrol with your clients new recon squad, personally trained by you or find yourself in the middle of nowhere after a plane crash, car breakdown or something like that.

As merc legend Frank Camper once stated: survival skills like finding and purifying water are not even remotely as sexy as advanced firearms or combatives training. Yet, considering your plans of working in places with, let's call it, „an infrastructure with room for improvement" this kind of skill is elemental – you're going to drink water way more often than you're going to shoot people.

So, knowing how to warm up a MRE (Meals ready-to-eat) is not even close to enough. Starting a fire even while heavy rain is falling, building a shelter, finding food and the mentioned water and not poisoning yourself consuming it as well as doing all of it while hiding from enemy patrols and a lot more... you are getting it, right?

So, start looking for basic survival courses in your country and take one. Again, do some prior research to get quality training for your bucks. Also, once you plan your first job, consider a second course that coverts he specific area you are moving to. Because that desert survival course in Arizona may turn out lack information needed once you arrive in the moist heat of the jungle or some snow-covered woodland in eastern Europe.

Combat Survival and SER-E (Survival, Evasion, Resistance & Escape) trainings are also becoming more and more available to the interested public. If you find a good course for those, take it. Ideally AFTER some initial basic survival training.

And one more thing: stay away from the entertainment

videos this time, Joe – especially the famous „survival stars "
tend to show lots of bullshit, getting you killed in real life. But
several good books are available if you want to gather some
knowledge before visiting your courses.

EMERGENCY MEDICINE

When working in a conflict environment or even simply in remote distance to civilization, skills in emergency medicine and tactical combat casualty care (TCCC) are nonnegotiable.

Just like fieldcraft survival skills, medical training is one of the assets that will most likely once safe your life or someone else's. So, don't think that having been to that eight hour first-aid class once is nearly enough. TCCC focuses heavily on increasing survivability of people with injuries common to combat, meaning severe bleedings, collapsed lungs originating from a punctured chest and the like. If you have been in any army, you most likely had at least some of that. If not, those courses are not uncommon on the market these days, giving civilians skills that may also save human life in case of a terrorist attack and former military medics a job to pay their bills. Speaking of that: being qualified to teach TCCC and other medical skills may be hell of a door opener for merc work because, guess what, a huge amount of third world forces don't have those yet, resulting in high counts of preventable losses.

But don't stay with just the combat medic stuff – that may be ok for the regular trigger-pullers that have their own MDs, ICUs and medevac-teams with them in any country they deploy to. A Marine gets some malaria and the doc will take care of it. GI Joe has eaten the wrong street food on leave and now his seemingly water-like shit is mixed with blood? Let the doc have a look on that!

You won't have this as a freelancer, or at least not always. So better have an answer for problems not related to combat, too. Because you also won't always have wi-fi to google your symptoms (and thereby learn you are beyond hope) either.

In many countries, you could sign up for paramedical training, meaning that for a small fee you will learn a huge lot of medical stuff, all focused on practical use. Not too many Latin here, Joe. Don't worry. Depending on where you do this you may even do some work at the ambulance, gathering experience on real people with real injuries, sicknesses and the like. Just don't expect this to not leave any marks on your heart and soul, cold-blooded merc or not. Having a small girl dying in front of you, his parents screaming, crying begging or threatening you, maybe all of it... welcome to the real world.

Yet, having the experience and knowledge to help yourself and others at anything ranging from a cold to a blown-of leg will increase your chances of survival as much as your value for any outfit you work with. And once more: value is something that gets PAID!

DRIVING AND VARIOUS VEHICLE HANDLING

Not being able to drive a car will be a huge problem when working in conflict zones. This does refer to a valid license but much more to the real skills. Remember, you are going to go to places others want to leave. So, if you can get hands on a vehicle, it won't have all the nice assistance systems most people are so used to today. Nor will you likely find anything with an automatic gearbox. So better know how to drive without anything else than a motor, a steering wheel and four tires if you're lucky. Three and a half if not.

Also being able to handle other means of transportation will come in handy, again meaning legally but much more technically. Different types of motorized bikes are common in the third world, as are different animals to ride and, depending the area, small boats moved by an engine. Being able to fly, no matter if it's a plane, a helicopter or even both, would be king level, but that's an expensive skill and not a necessity.

If you opt for close protection, learning to drive evasive as well as work with armored cars is imperative, given you don't plan to move your VIP in a nice BMW that couldn't stop a 9mm through Kabul, Baghdad or any other nice little town. Most outfits have special designated drivers – until they get sick or shot in the worst possible moment.

LANGUAGES

Without some higher command sorting out travel, supplies
and all the other details for you, some knowledge of the local
language is a valuable asset. Also, you are not going to share
barracks with some platoons of your own nationality. You are
a hired gun, a sole operative as you may remember.
So, doing your job will require interaction with the locals you
are working for. And that includes talking. Even if your POC
(Point of Contact) is doing well with English – you are there to
support them, not annoy your POC by asking him to
accompany you as your personal translator all the time.

If you already started to cringe at the idea of having to learn a
language or *sigh* more than one – worry not.

You probably remember the terrible language classes back in
your school and trying to learn all those grammar rules and
stuff. No need for that, you learn for Merc work, not a test.

The easiest way is to use one of the many language apps out
there, right in your smartphones Appstore! Unlike your
classes in school, these are designed using up-to-date
knowledge about how people learn languages. And that is
NOT by grammar rules. You are going to focus on important
words rather than details.

If you want to, you may also visit a language course at any of
the many schools that exist out there. If you plan to work
with PMCs or other "official" companies, go for one issuing
you an official certification on your learned skill for your CV.

Knowing to order fries in Oman is nice, a certification saying
you have Level B1 in Arab is better. That certificate issued by
a school with international reputation would be best.

And don't worry, the private schools won't try the shitty kind
of language teaching you may remember from school neither.
They want to prevail on the free market too, meaning they
work in a more efficient and fun way.

So, no matter if app, school or both – languages, at least
basics, are nonnegotiable. Even if you initially sound like
Master Yoda from Star Wars – the locals will get your
message and most of the time they are really humbled when
a foreigner bothers to learn their language.
Building on your basic words and daily use of the language,
you will make rapid progress. Together with your language,
you will also improve your understanding of the area, the
peoples traditions and specifics and much more.
We will sort this out later in detail, but compare that to any
combat soldier, having been deployed to no matter where.
How much knowledge of culture, languages and other
important stuff does he have to offer if, say, some smaller
company needs to do business in that area. If you, as that
customer, needed to not only be protected from harm but
also from doing severe mistakes and ruin that relationship –
who would YOU hire?

Reading

Yes, more nerd stuff. I know that having to bother that pretty brain of yours with languages was a hard pill to swallow, but … reading? Like you're doing right now, assuming you're not having some app (or your mom) reading this to you?

Yes. And a lot. To quote Paul Balor, one of the most successful mercs of the last decades, once more:

"Professionals in this business are a highly literate crew. They read voraciously."

Better believe it. As long as you don't want to spend your life as a lowest-level trigger-puller (meaning lowest-level payment and life-expectancy, too), reading will make a real big difference. And I'm not talking about that pulp-fiction love-novels you hide under your bed!
A course on Speedreading may be one of the wisest investments in your life – so better take one soon. Afterwards, you may want to train your new skill on some stuff:

First of all, all things on the "mercenary" topic should be interesting to you, even if outdated. History tends to repeat itself to those who don't learn from it. So, get an overview of the history of our occupation. Also, the classic manuals from the 80s are worth a read. Have a look in the appendix for more info's on that.

Reading the news should be your normal from now on, even if the mainstream media is, of course, not objective or even true on many things. Nobody expects you to believe anything you read. But know what's going on – and what is told to the public. No matter if you guess that politicians control the media or the media controls the public and thereby, indirectly, the politics… there is no tin-foil-hat factor in seeing that the mass-media IS having some control on the developments. So, it's YOUR job to watch it and make use of it.

If, say, you tend to read about a certain lands or militias "grueling war crimes" more and more often, better expect something to go on over there quite soon and maybe even start studying the area, language and other players in that conflict. You may soon find work there.

Books, blogs and magazines on guns, war, combatives and the like are obvious choices.

For blogs, check out at least these two:

https://gabesuarez.com/
Gabe is a seasoned firearms & tactics instructor, Karate blackbelt and former police officer that once killed three gangers in a gunfight – a fact he often refers to in his classes, books and articles.
Also, he is a great believer in the development of warriors and thereby putting his experience as a gunfighter, street cop and Karate-sensei online in his very unique posts. Post you may find racist, offensive or over-paced – but ol' Gabe definitely has a point on many things from certain shooting techniques, knife use in the real world and training tools like force-on-force up to the "warrior lifestyle "philosophy and the topic of killing itself that may be interesting for you. He certainly is a unique guy (so are most in this way of life. You will not find too many "easy characters" amongst those who work in this world) and worth listening to, even if you don't

agree with all of his religious and political statements. He certainly wouldn't give a fuck on your opinion, I'm sure.

https://www.edsmanifesto.com/blog

Ed was in the Mexican special forces and travels the world now, mainly doing "advisory" work for clients and courses on personal security, focused on freeing from unlawful custody, surviving in an urban environment and improvising weapons. If this sounds a little "merc" … well. One more reason to study that guy! To give you two impressions on HOW this guy works:

1.) the "Fruit Knife concept"

Given the fact that most of us can't bring any defensive means with them, Ed worked out a solution: the Victorinox Fruit knife is sharp as hell, cheap and legal almost all over the world. By bringing a kydex-holster with him (innocent piece of plastic to any customs official) now he is armed with a handy and expendable last-ditch option if some cake, salami or motherfucker needs to be sliced.

Just notice that the fruit knife with a slightly curved, short blade works perfectly with Libre and especially its "Reaper method". Other styles of knife fighting may not work that well with this kind of knife. So, you may have to adapt his idea to fit your needs.

2.) Listerine

The famous mouthwash is good for dental hygiene and dental hygiene is good to be efficient when engaged in a foreign war. That's obvious.

Little less known is that Listerine also serves great for disinfecting wounds all over the body. It's a universal, cheap and readily available asset for the traveler going to places where pharmacies are not too common – but injuries and infections are.

These two guys are at the time of this being written also present on Facebook and Instagram and posting there even more stuff. So, grab a drink and fill some hours sucking up knowledge, taking notes and have a laugh or two, for both guys also have a unique sense of humor.

Many other guys also have blogs, sites and even YouTube channels – the good as well as the bad and the ugly.

Pat McNamarra was mentioned before. His "Combat Strength Training" being present on Facebook and Instagram as well as Youtube. Get some impressions of his style at
https://www.youtube.com/user/patannamac1
His books "Sentinel" and "T.A.P.S." are also worth your time and effort! They are available on amazon.com for kindle, one of the greatest tools for the traveler. More on this in the next Volume again.

Scott Babbs **Libre** as a style of vicious knife fighting was mentioned before, too. Here you can get some better idea of how it works:
https://www.youtube.com/user/LibreFighting

Again: a lot of the curriculum these days is over-fancy, for they orient more and more on customers joining the training for the thrill of it, not focused on the real-world application. So, don't bother to learn six different ways to attack an eye, but identify the one for you and try to find a trainer who got the original "Reaper" stuff. Nothing better exists if you want to develop a reality-ready knife skill.

Lee Morrisons "Urban Combatives" is a close ally of Libre and a great source on realistic combatives. It is made up for civilians in street defense, sure but be assured it works as well with a vest on.

https://www.youtube.com/channel/UCtfZTdRCfEoRYRqzBUur3lA

Also remember that H2H skill is also wanted for the times where you are not supposed to shoot people, meaning your recovery times, traveling and also disputes with other guys on your side. Yapp, this DOES happen at times and even if you may really feel like doing so, shooting one of your own guys will ruin your career and life 95% of the time!

Kelly McCann is another name to look for, having been a Marine, CIA operative, freelance "security advisor" and one of Lee Morrisons trainers. He is an impressive warrior and his videos and even more his books are a must for anybody working in the field of warfare, danger and taking lives.

These are the most important guys to start with in persuasion of a professional warrior's life. But, again, your research and learning should NOT be focused on the "tacticool" mercenary stuff only!
Also think about subjects like taxes & finances, especially when it comes to payment in other countries. Diplomacy, persuasion, sales and manipulation including the great skills included in the "social engineering" framework will help you for sure out there as well as some books covering the broad subject of OSINT research and everything related to international travel. And put those last two into action before you book a flight, as long as you plan for a return!

MORE TRAINING TO CONSIDER
You should be aware of a common trap to "never feel ready"
and doing training after training, but never go out there and
do what you train for.
"Better done than perfect" is a nice saying that pretty much
sums it up.
Yet as I told you before, rushing of with too little preparation
may also not be a healthy idea.

So, don't spend all your lifetime and money on all available
training but make a plan what you need and follow that plan.

If you are not used to travel internationally (and again, your
military deployments DON'T count! All was sorted out for
you, from flights, visa and transportation up to
communications and healthcare!), a course or two on **Travel
Security** will pay off in more than one way! You will learn a lot
on common crime and problems people encounter when in
foreign lands. Good courses will also cover the subjects of
bribery (common in most countries we work in, yet a delicate
subject. Refuse to pay a bribe there and sure get into trouble.
Be too obvious in bribing someone and get even more) and
other interactions with the officials, putting together an
escape-set, how to most likely survive a carjacking or street
robbery, securing a hotel room and reasons to do so and
much more. If you chose the right course, your teacher is
likely to be a former soldier or spook with some personal
experience. - so, listen closely!
Also, a good reason for that kind of course: the other people
usually will be from small and middle-class businesses
working internationally – otherwise, their company would
have a training of its own. Don't think GM or Apple will send
their guys to some open course. So, you're in class with future

customers! More on how to use this in Vol. 2, just a hint: don't introduce yourself as a mercenary in class and hand out flyers having "you pay, I slay" written on top of a skull logo with two crossed AK-47s in the coffee break... may not work the way you planed. Yes, that includes this book's logo as well – but remember, this book is not meant to attract average Joe and Emma.

Finally, this kind of courses may be something to do yourself in the future, so write down all you can for a possible later use. Again, details in the next volumes. Hey, I need to pay my bills too.

Courses on **international business laws** and **tax management / avoidance** may pay of soon in lower taxes, unless you get paid tax free anyways (like blood diamonds and bitcoin). Yet I suggest you don't, because it's a little stupid to survive a foreign war only to get arrested for tax violations back home. So, better get some knowledge on this topic. You may even work up to becoming fully transnational and not pay ANY taxes on income at all, but the interesting this sounds, the complicated it is and the costs to set this kind of thing up are often higher than your total income, at least in the first few years. Yet, we will look more deeply at this option in Vol. III as it may be interesting in the later years of your career.

Training in **sales and persuasion** may come in handy for someone selling his service to different customers. Just a thought...

IT security is something to also know at least a little about when you travel to places where you may suddenly face problems to access your account that holds some information that just this second turned out to be vital. Knowing about

what a government can trace back and how, using TOR and
the dark web and untraceable e-mails is nothing you need a
master's degree in IT for.
If you happen to own the latter, you may soon face a rather
huge market in front of you. Options for cyber-mercs follow …
you guessed it: in Vol. II.

Research and OSINT skills, observation, lockpicking, poisons
and other tradecraft / cloack&dagger stuff are also interesting
in this trade and if you feel like knowing more, go ahead.
So are the great courses on **counter custody, improvised
weapons** and **surviving in an urban environment** by the
exceptional Ed Calderon mentioned above, if you happen to
be able to join one.

You may have recognized that a lot of recommendations
double, being mentioned in "reading" as well as "courses to
take". That's true and it is up to you to consider what topics
to cover by reading, getting hands-on instruction or even
ignore because you estimate yourself to be fit in that subject
or consider it irrelevant. Well, you're a freelancer and that's
up to you. Don't say I didn't warn you.

Final words

The first volume of our guide has come to an end by now and you may be biting fingernails awaiting the next one. Worry not, you won't have to wait too long. Maybe you're reading this in a not-too-distant future and Vol. II starts on the next pages of the "full collection edition".

If not, don't worry – you've got enough homework for now to keep you busy until Vol. II is released.

Minding the fact that you don't want to just do some merc work but also survive, improve and be able to live from the money you earn instead of getting killed, crippled or returning home broke and live on other people's money you hopefully start right now, if you didn't start yet, to acquire the skills and knowledge to become a valuable asset for both your customers and the men next to you in combat.

How to make money selling these hard-learned skills to the highest bidder?

Who may be your customers?

How do you market yourself the right way?

How to find your personal, specific market?

How to prepare for your first deployment?

What to buy and bring there? Are several thousand bucks on tactical clothing and equipment to look like fresh out of the latest "Call-of-Duty" game really necessary?

What kind of knife is the best to buy? (feels like one of the most common questions out there)

How, and where, can you build more contacts - paying off in even more and better work?

And probably the BIGGEST of all: ***How can I enter this mysterious, exciting, lucrative and shadowy world of hired guns, military advisors, spies and black-ops operators?***

All of those questions will be answered in detail including detailed descriptions of how highly trained specialists as well as adventurers without any relevant background made it on the inside. Including sources to learn more on them. You may feel annoyed now for these were the questions you hoped to find answered in this volume.

Well, look again, this was never claimed.

Yes, of course I also do this to sell more books – remember, selling my skills, knowledge and experience for MONEY, not thankful thoughts, is my business, too.

But also, I want to minimize the amount of people skipping the "boring" parts and just read the "how to get inside" parts, go ahead and get killed. Nothing can totally prevent this, but I still feel better taking precautions.

So, start working out 'till you puke. Shoot until your hands have small blisters that eventually start bleeding, tape these spots and shoot some more. Get beaten up by your partners, start beating up your partners while sparring, but also practice breakfalls, breaking holds, disarming people trying to intimidate or even kill you with their weapons and lack of competence using them (sorry, virtually no way to disarm a pro).

Recover from all this torture in your armchair, reading the suggested books and blogs and stream the recommended videos on you giant 65" TV while having a cold one or two.

Visit some seminars, start to make contact with like-minded people and see what additional tips they have on books, videos, courses and the like.

Still, stay aware of all the scams and rip-offs out there. If you like, have a look at some of the more successful of them (you'll find them in the progress of your training, don't worry) and see what they use to sell themselves. Who are their customers and what needs do the scammers address?

Check our trades illustrious history, from the most ancient times, the Varangians and Jomsvikings, passing the 30 years' war and war of independence in the USA to finally the era between WW 2 and today. Ever heard of Mike Hoare or Siegfried "Kongo Mueller" Mueller?

Finally, keep your eyes on the ever-evolving scene of conflicts all over the world. What is happening where and why. Check the official, proclaimed reasons and, if you can sort out, the covered real ones as well. So, to make it short: make use of your waiting time by becoming a devoted student of the second-oldest profession of mankind. Transform yourself into a warrior, a tool of death and destruction, that is worth to be hired and capable to survive, even when uncertainty and disaster strike – because for sure, they will!

And never forget to ENJOY all of that! If you can't find fun, joy and excitement in these trainings and studies, think about your choice of working in this profession once more, and properly.

On the other hand: if you love very single second of these activities, be assured that the things you prepare for will be even greater, more exciting and more rewarding! Keep going!

So, it's goodbye for now, until next time, Joe Merc - and watch 'ur 6. You've started to walk a way of life that will get you enemies quite soon and more than enough! And not all of them will be kind enough to show their intentions by shooting in your direction. Be aware!

Yours sincerely, as a brother in arms!

Chris

APPENDIX A — TOP-10 BOOKS FOR THE MERCENARY IN TRAINING

1. Manual of the mercenary soldier – Paul Balor
THE classic book of the trade, stuffed with information and insights as well as a second-to-none style of writing.

2. Live to spend it – Frank Camper
Basically the legendary RECONDO merc schools course, transformed to be applied from your couch.

3. Combatives for street survival - Kelly McCann
Coming in a set with three DVDs, this will give you a very good idea of the skills needed. Also, if you can't find any good realworld training to put on top of your recommended basic boxing and grappling skills, this will guide you in how to start a study group of likeminded individuals.

4. Save the last bullet for yourself – Rob Krott
A true mercenaries report on his various assignments, starting in the US special forces and ranging from training recon teams in the Kosovo to high-paid military contracting in Africa.

5. Street Smarts, Firearms, & Personal Security – Jim Grover (aka Kelly McCann)
A collection of articles written by Kelly under his old pen name on virtually every topic regarding personal security. Old, but gold.

6. Sentinel – Pat McNamarra
Insights on different aspects of personal security by a former

Delta-operator. Focused heavily on civilians, yet useful for our kind as well

7. T.A.P.S. – Pat McNamarra
A very good work on reality-focused firearms training by the same guy.

8. Fighting ISIS – Tim Locks
A former corrections officer & bouncer that joined the war against the so-called "Islamic-state" in Syria and Iraq. Good example of a Soldier of Fortune without any military background.

9. Social Engineering - Christopher Hadnagy
Working in this job means working with different people and also depending on some, ranging from customers of your service to police or airport officials that have to decide if you're a problem or not. Knowing how to "play" people may become a skill you use more often than your 100 yard off-hand pistol shot.

10. Rich dad, poor dad – Robert Kyosaki
Not including anything needed to fight in foreign wars, it still got on the list for offering another skill too many in our trade lack – to keep some of the money you earn. Make sure you don't survive all the madness of this job only to end up old and completely broke. Remember, being a Mercenary is about war AND money – so better get some skills with the latter as well!

APPENDIX B — WEBSITES WORTH A LOOK

1. http://shooterjobs.com
Basically a collection of open jobs in armed international work.
Founder is one of the few guys in the industry that don't cringe
about the word mercenary. He even sells merc-merchandise.

2. https://www.pmci.online/
Online-magazine covering many subjects all around armed
overseas work. Feels a little like the old "SoF" and "Gung-Ho"
issues, of course prevents terms like "Mercenary", "Soldier of
Fortune" or "Gun for hire".

3. http://navyseals.com/wp-
content/uploads/2012/12/naval-special-warfare-physical-
training-guide.pdf
Training guide for people interested to apply for "Basic Underwater
Demolitions / SEAL" training in the US Navy. If you ignore all the
swimming, its still a great guide to get in fighting-shape.

4. http://nononsenseselfdefense.com/
Grab a coffee before you go on this one – LOTS of text!
Still the ultimate knowledgebase regarding the realities of combat,
violence & fear.

5. https://gabesuarez.com/
As mentioned in the book: seasoned firearms & tactics
instructor, Karate blackbelt and former police officer. Extreme
amount of free content.

6. https://www.edsmanifesto.com/blog
Also got mentioned in the book but worth to be mentioned
again, too. A world-class expert in low-budget, down-and-

dirty stuff, ranging from lockpicking and countering custody to improvising weapons, knife combatives and combat survival in a hostile urban environment.

7. http://www.combatstrengthtraining.com/
Former DELTA-guy offering a top-level fitness concept for a reasonable price. Highly recommended!

8. https://tgace.wordpress.com/category/tactical-preschool/
Quite LE-focused site, yet some interesting topics and scenarios getting covered.